Raising Sexually Healthy Kids

....

David White

New
Growth
Press

www.newgrowthpress.com

New Growth Press, Greensboro, NC 27404
www.newgrowthpress.com
Copyright © 2014 by Harvest USA

All Scripture quotations, unless otherwise indicated are from *The
Holy Bible, English Standard Version*® (ESV®), copyright © 2000,
2001 by Crossway Bibles, a division of Good News Publishers.
Used by permission. All rights reserved.
   Scripture quotations marked NIV are taken from the *Holy
Bible,* New International Version®, NIV®. Copyright © 1973, 1978,
1984, 2011 by Biblica, Inc. Used by permission. All rights reserved
worldwide.

Cover Design: Faceout Books, faceoutstudio.com
Typesetting: Lisa Parnell, Thompson's Station, TN

ISBN: 978-1-939946-86-7 (Print)
ISBN: 978-1-939946-87-4 (eBook)

Library of Congress Cataloging-in-Publication Data
White, David, 1970–
  Raising sexually healthy kids / David White.
      pages cm
  ISBN 978-1-939946-86-7 (print) — ISBN 978-1-939946-87-4
(ebook) 1. Sex—Religious aspects—Christianity. 2. Sex instruction for children—Religious aspects—Christianity. 3. Child rear-
ing—Religious aspects—Christianity. 4. Parenting—Religious
aspects—Christianity. I. Title.
  BT708.W429 2014
  248.8'45—dc23

                                                          2014026146

Printed in Canada

21 20 19 18 17 16 15 14   1 2 3 4 5

An anti-drug commercial opened with a middle school student innocently walking in the door after school, only to discover the dining room table covered with sex education materials—including scale models! The father casually suggests they could talk about drugs instead, if the child preferred. Though humorous, the commercial poignantly illustrates a sad reality: sex is the last topic kids and parents want to discuss.

This has been a problem for a long time. I regularly ask church audiences to raise their hands if they learned about sexuality from their parents. Typically less than 10 percent respond, and most of those were just handed a book. It is tragic that this crucial area of life and obedience is so sorely neglected in most Christian homes. Even when discussion does occur it tends to focus on the mundane—basic mechanics and abstinence—and neglect the glory and ecstasy of God's design and the wondrous truth that human sexuality is profoundly theological.

The last thing we want to discuss

Talking to your kids about sexuality is more important now than ever before. Sex is one of the biggest idols in our culture. Everything from the sensual images on billboards to celebrities on primetime TV bombard us daily with the message that sex is all-important. Our children are not oblivious to these messages and images. But, particularly at younger ages, our kids desperately need our help to interpret these messages and images, and they need us to teach them sexuality from the Scriptures.

With the legislative approval of same-sex marriage, your elementary-age children will likely befriend students with two moms or dads. Many of us already encounter this issue in our extended families or neighborhoods. And this is true for each stage of development: your older kids need shepherding to love their LGBTQ friends, while their "hearts honor Christ the Lord as holy, always being prepared to make a defense to anyone who asks [them] for a reason for the hope that is in [them] . . . with gentleness and respect" (1 Peter 3:15). And overall, the rapid advance of technology means that our children face unprecedented risk to temptation and sexual predators. Tragically, with the ease of its availability, I've encountered children as young as six years old addicted to Internet pornography. As parents, we need to be the first people to talk to our children about sexuality. It is profoundly unloving to leave them to the darkness of the world's answers or the folly of their peers.

We are woefully neglecting God's calling as parents if we fail to address these issues from a biblical perspective. Our most significant role is to pass on the faith to our children, providing a biblical worldview and helping our kids understand their lives in the story of God's redemption. We are actors in his drama, who by grace have a role in extending his kingdom. Just as in the first-century Greco-Roman world, the twenty-first-century American church has the opportunity to be radically countercultural by honoring Christ with our sexuality in a sexually insane culture. Our children need to be trained, and this begins when we step out of our comfort zones to risk the dreaded conversation.

Start with Yourself

How do you speak to your kids about sex? Begin by looking inward. Instilling a healthy understanding of sexuality in your child starts with *you* addressing ways your own perspective may be warped by past (or current!) sinful experience, sexual abuse, or unbiblical thinking about sex.

Here are some things to think about before you talk to your kids:

- Do you believe God created our sexuality and declares it "very good"? How might your unspoken attitudes communicate a different message to your kids? Do you believe God smiles upon the lovemaking of a husband and wife? Why or why not?

- All of us have a sexuality affected by our own lust and the lies of the world. How have Hollywood, romance novels, or pornography impacted you? One way to gauge this is to be honest about your frustration or disappointment in this area of life. How do you feel God has "let you down" sexually? What would make for a great sex life?

- Because of my sexual history prior to marriage, for many years I felt shame about intimacy with my wife, even though I knew intellectually that it was blessed by God. Were you sexually active before marriage or did you struggle with porn and solo sex? Although you may now be faithful to your spouse, past sexual sin can affect the way we think and respond to our children. Do you tend to minimize or overlook your children's behavior (e.g., having a "boys will be boys" attitude about pornography)? Do you feel hypocritical challenging your child's relationships, either fearing or knowing they are sexual, because of your own past sexual failures? Or are you too strict, placing heavy burdens to stifle your child's social life because of your past failures?

- Many of us live with a sexuality scarred by another's exploitation. If this is you, please seek the care of a competent, *experienced* Christian counselor to help you find healing. There is no greater trauma than sexual abuse, so even if it occurred decades ago, don't assume it hasn't impacted your soul.

- Where do you struggle with sexuality *today*? Does anyone in your life know? Are you willing to bring it "into the light"? You will only be able to overcome private struggles with sin if you are willing to humble yourself and ask others for help. We do not experience significant change in any sin struggle unless we bring it into the open with others in the body of Christ because this is how God calls us to live (see 1 Corinthians 12:12–26; Ephesians 4:11–16; Colossians 2:19).

Know this: your sexuality will impact your kids. Your growth in this area will enable your kids to gain wisdom and understand how sexuality fits into the broader issues of Christian living. Conversely, reluctance to examine your heart (or worse, ongoing sexual sin) will be detrimental to your children. The Bible shows us that children learn to worship the "household gods" of their parents (Joshua 24:14–15; Jeremiah 7:18). The hard truth is our idols are passed on to our kids! Is there sexual sin in your life that you are hiding from your spouse and others in the body of Christ? Know that who you are sexually reveals who you are spiritually (see Ephesians 4:17–19; 1 Thessalonians 4:3–8). If we want our children to have a holy awe and delight for this good gift, we need to take our personal sexual integrity seriously and grow in our realization that God rejoices when we cherish and honor him with our sexuality.

You don't need to have everything figured out from your own past before you begin shepherding your child's sexuality. You don't need to be perfect in this area of life. But as you teach your kids about God's wonderful design for sexuality, don't neglect the work that is still needed in your own life. You will grow in grace as you lead your children into the grace of Christ.

Start Positive

Too often the church is silent about sex. If there is teaching, it tends to be abstinence programs aimed at the youth, with a focus on the negatives: unwanted pregnancy, STDs, etc. The church desperately needs to communicate a positive theology of sexuality. Sex was God's idea, and he declared it to be "very good." The ecstasy of sex is by design. God concentrated the nerve endings in our genitals. He crafted the glorious intensity of an orgasm. Sex is a good gift he invites us to delight in! The Song of Solomon is a "God-breathed" celebration of human sexuality. Historically the church has allegorized this book, confining it to a description of Christ and the church. Even modern interpreters can be a little gun-shy. For example, our English translations make accurate, but very "safe" decisions in rendering the Hebrew—which would make most of us blush.[1]

Briefly, God created humanity male and female as his "image-bearers." When Eve was taken out of Adam, the single human was (in a sense) split in half. Hence, Adam's joyful declaration, "This at last is bone of my bones and flesh of my flesh; she shall be called Woman, because she was taken out of Man" (Genesis 2:23). The ecstasy of sexuality is intended to give us a snapshot of the wonder of being made in the image of God. Consider: God's image that was split into two sexes is physically brought back together in the sexual union. It is a "reunion" of God's complementary image—in the very act of creating! Why does this matter? We worship a Trinitarian God, existing in eternal relationship. In sexuality, God gives us a tiny glimpse—as in a mirror dimly—into the joy and delight experienced within the Trinity. Human sexuality is a place where God declares to his creation, "I Am!"

But it goes even deeper. Marriage and sexuality ultimately point us to our relationship with Christ. In discussing marital roles, Ephesians 5 comes to a startling crescendo, "This mystery is profound, and I am saying that it refers to Christ and the church" (v. 32). One of the reasons God created marriage is for us to know the depth of his love for us. Although often depicted negatively in the Prophets (Israel as adulteress, God as faithful husband), there are also many glorious expressions: "For as a young man marries a young woman, so shall your sons marry you, and as the bridegroom rejoices over the bride, so shall your God rejoice over you" (Isaiah 62:5). "'In that day,' declares the LORD, 'you will call me "my husband"; you will no longer call me "my master"'" (Hosea 2:16 NIV). "The LORD your God is in your midst, a mighty one who will save; he will rejoice over you with gladness; he will quiet you by his love; he will exult over you with loud singing" (Zephaniah 3:17).

Marriage at its best is intended to point us to Jesus's joy and delight in his people. The sexual longing of a husband and wife for one another is a glimpse at Jesus's longing for the coming wedding feast of the Lamb. This wondrous reality is part of the reason sexuality is reserved for marriage: God commands a husband and wife to complete physical and emotional fidelity to give us a picture of the importance of our complete spiritual fidelity to Jesus. He wants all of our love and devotion. He will not share us with rival lovers. As this brief sketch reveals, there is much more to tell your kids about God's design than "wait until you're married."

The idea of covenant is central here. Our culture bases decisions off feelings, so that "love" is reduced to warm, fuzzy emotions toward another. This is the sandy relational foundation for many, so when the feelings dissipate, the relationship ends. Biblically speaking, love is always an action that selflessly moves toward others. Thus, God's design for sex is rooted in *promises:* a pledged, lifelong commitment. Sex is a gift received on the back end of that promise, part of the blessings a couple experience after commitment. God knows it is only safe to be naked and unashamed physically, not to mention emotionally and spiritually, within the context of that promise.

Further, sex is limited to this pledged relationship because God never intended sex to be merely a recreational activity detached from procreation. That's clear from the beginning of Genesis. Though we live in a post-Fall world where infertility is a painful issue for many couples and some older couples marry after childbearing years, the connection between sex and children remains. Marriage has been the cornerstone of nearly every society, and it could be argued that traditional marriage is the most successful social construct in history. God's design for human sexuality isn't just to reveal theological truth, but to safeguard adults, children, and society as a whole. Sadly, many sexual partners do not marry. And too often marriages fail. By God's grace, many children raised by a single parent grow up healthy and well-adjusted, but the principle remains—God's design for sex is intended for this covenantal relationship because a two-parent family with a mom and dad is the best environment for childrearing.

Do It Together

When possible, husbands and wives should engage their kids together. This assumes a couple will discuss things prior to the initial conversation and establish a mutually agreed upon strategy. Prayerfully be prepared to answer when the questions start coming. Why is this important? Candid conversation demonstrates that in God's design, shame does not accompany sexuality. When sexual conversation is restricted to the same-sex parent it fosters misunderstanding, especially in a home where every other subject is readily discussed as a family. Treating sexuality as a natural, healthy aspect of Christian living is the beginning of the best sexual education you can offer your child.

This provides an additional challenge for single parents. Prayerfully consider who can assist you in this process. Do you have wise members of your extended family? Are you a part of a home Bible study or have close Christian friends who can come alongside you? Although sexuality was very openly discussed in our home from the time my daughters were young, when my first wife died, I was very blessed to have other women step in and care for them in areas I couldn't as a man. This poignantly underscores the importance of living the Christian life rooted in the body of Christ. At a time when society is increasingly fractured, having a strong community of faith is more important than ever, and it is a powerful witness to a watching world.

Start Small

How do you speak to kids about sex? Too many parents wait for that one-time, preteen, gut-wrenching conversation. But if you wait until your child is ten to twelve years old to talk about sex, they will likely have already learned from another source. That said, it is never too late. If you waited to talk to your preteen, start now!

Ideally, rather than a single, dreaded ordeal, sexual conversations should begin early and continue throughout the child's life. Many parents are wary of creating an unhealthy interest in sexuality. This is wise, but you must be prepared to speak. When your child begins to ask questions, it is obvious that he is ready for accurate, age-appropriate answers.

At four, my twin girls began asking questions about pregnancy and my late wife explained that God made a "special hug" for mommies and daddies to enjoy and that sometimes this makes a baby. For that conversation, at that time, her response was enough. Be forewarned: after I shared this with a friend she talked similarly to her kids, and they asked to watch! But even this provides a great opportunity to continue the conversation about appropriate boundaries with sexuality. Here you could explain that it is inappropriate for children to see their parents' "special hug" because it is a private thing that God made just for them.

As your children become more aware of physical gender differences, begin to discuss the mechanics more specifically and use the technical terms for body parts. Again, take advantage of natural inroads. I remember drawing a school of squiggly sperm and an ovum on a napkin at the dinner table. You don't have to go overboard in detail when they are young. Allow their questions to dictate the depth of the discussion. Starting young is easier on everyone. A child who has no shameful associations with sex or his genitals makes the conversation less embarrassing for the parents as well.

Further, it is imperative to speak to your children at the earliest possible age about inappropriate touching. As soon as my children were able to understand, even before they were able to speak, I explained to them that only mommy and daddy were allowed to take off their diaper, bathe them, etc. Children need to be taught to establish physical boundaries with others and to talk to you if anyone attempts to touch them inappropriately. An important step here is allowing your child to have a "voice" regarding his body. This means not forcing him to hug Great Aunt Gertrude who he's never met, or sit on a neighbor's lap if it makes him uncomfortable. This means even honoring the cry to "Stop!" despite their laughter when you're tickling them. These simple steps begin to teach them that they have a say in what happens to their body. They also need to be instructed not to touch others' private areas. These conversations are so important because typically, in the grooming process, perpetrators tell children no one will believe them if they reveal the abuse. Be proactive and communicate that you will believe your child if he discloses inappropriate touching. Even this discussion can be a low-level introduction to God's design, explaining that he made our genitals with a special function to be shared only with our future spouse. Sadly, in most cases, the perpetrator is a family member, caretaker, or trusted friend, so you must be wary.

Facing the Curse

As your child moves through elementary school, it is important to start explaining ways that sexuality is affected by the Fall. After our first parents rebelled, everything created "very good" became tainted. Although there is still much blessing in the world because of God's common grace, all aspects of life are affected by sin and need redemption.

I was exposed to pornography at a friend's house around age four or five. And life has radically changed since the '70s. Because of the explosion of technology (computers, Internet, smartphones, tablets, iPods, and game systems), our kids have access to porn so graphic it would have been unavailable in adult bookstores a generation ago. I regularly receive calls from parents whose children have accessed extreme forms of online pornography. One man shared how his four-year-old unwittingly ordered an adult film off Pay-Per-View. Some kids are hooked on Internet porn by the age of six.

In addition to online pornography, there is also relentless daily bombardment of sensuality in virtually every form of media your child encounters. Obviously you want to avoid sensual images, but pay attention to your child's response to the magazines in the grocery store or displays at the mall. If you notice her reading magazine covers, ask her in the car on the way home if she read anything confusing that she didn't understand. Be willing to talk to your child about images if you noticed her gaze lingering.

We also need to help even young children understand people whose sexual expression is outside God's boundaries. Many of us have family members in same-sex relationships. Increasingly, children in public schools will encounter all types of non-traditional families. The pervasive pro-gay messages from the media have dramatically impacted people's perceptions of homosexuality—including our children's. Consider that for their entire life today's kids have watched TV with nearly every program portraying homosexuality and same-sex relationships as normal. I understand parents are worried about telling their child too much too soon, but the sad reality is most parents wait and say too little far too late.

Public school will present a variety of challenges. You must be prepared to answer your child who befriends the kid with same-sex parents. Drawing from recent sins in your child's life (and your own), explain again that we all struggle to follow God even when we know him, and that people who don't know him often live in ways that are very different than his design. These conversations should be marked with compassion! Similar to the explanation of chaos in Judges 17:6; 21:25, explain to your child when there is "no king . . . everyone does what is right in his own eyes." Increasingly, school curricula teach unbiblical principles at younger and younger ages. Parents should *always* do everything they can to know what is being taught to their young children and be ready to help identify things that go against the truth of the Bible. You don't need to fear the lies of the world, but you *do* need to be ready to counter them! For example, a significant cultural argument is that it doesn't matter who you "love." Using passages like 1 Corinthians 13 and 1 John 5:2–3, this is a great opportunity to contrast the Bible's radically countercultural definition of love against the gooey, self-focused emotion extolled by Hollywood.

The media splash over the Colorado courts upholding the rights of a transgendered six-year-old is a snapshot of where things are headed nationally. How will you shepherd your child through this? Will you encourage your kids to befriend such a person, or respond with contemptuous self-righteousness? I am grieved by reports of Christians pushing back against anti-bullying policies in schools seeking to protect the LGBTQ community. Is this the battle Jesus calls us to fight? I have ministered to countless men with same-sex attraction over the years, and literally all of them were called gay or queer before they even knew what it meant. (Often by kids in the church youth group.) We need to aggressively battle that kind of labeling. Christian kids should be at the forefront of loving those with radically different worldviews. And it is up to their parents to equip them and "spur [them] on to love and good deeds" (Hebrews 10:24 NIV). In the midst of all these discussions, be sure to keep at the center your hope in Christ and his redemption of broken things! Our kids should be encouraged to play Legos and have tea parties with others, even if they have parents of the same gender. How else will our children learn the importance of being "salt and light" in their cultural context?

What about concerns over your own child? Many parents are worried about effeminate boys or tomboy girls. First, remember that this has always been an issue! In fifth grade, my sister was the biggest kid in her class and a bruiser in neighborhood football games. Now she is married and a proud mother. What has become a huge concern to many parents was a non-issue years ago. Talk to your kids! Find out how they feel about their gender and how they're getting along with peers. In a world where gender is becoming something we decide, affirm the goodness of their created gender and God's intentionality in making them male or female. At the same time, celebrate their giftedness—don't force a musical or artistic boy to play basketball. Don't keep an active, athletic girl in an apron in the kitchen. Above all, don't shame them for behaviors that seem to "cross the line." Most of these issues resolve themselves as kids mature toward puberty and your overreaction or shaming can have a very detrimental effect.

Consider that "masculine" and "feminine" are not biblical categories, but culturally defined and even fluid between different cultures. David wrote much of the

Psalter, but was a warrior king greatly revered by his men. Deborah was a warrior and leader of God's people, but also a wife and likely a mother. We need to be careful not to push for cultural stereotypes when our ultimate goal is that our children be conformed to the image of Jesus.

This is a place where the role of the same-sex parent is extremely important. If your child resists embracing traditional activities, the same-sex parent should meet them where they are. A sensitive, fearful boy shouldn't be forced to impale a worm on a hook, no matter how ridiculous that seems to his father. How you respond to him is crucial in forming his sense of male identity. If he doesn't prefer your activities, do something he wants to do! What matters most is spending quality time together and affirming the person God created him (or her) to be.

Ironically, some parents' desperation to conform their child to traditional roles can have the opposite effect, making their child feel even more different and abnormal. This is another place where single parents need the assistance of the body of Christ. In homes where the same-sex parent is absent, these issues may be even more pronounced. Children always do best when raised in a community and, from my experience, there is particular urgency when we are single parenting!

As your child becomes a teen

Although beginning with family-wide conversations, as children approach puberty it is appropriate to begin gender-specific instruction about bodily changes, masturbation, etc. Again, single parents must recruit the help of other godly adults to participate in this crucial season of their child's life.

The teen years provide a wondrous opportunity for parents to begin gender-specific conversations that are more honest and vulnerable. Proverbs 5–7 presents a great blueprint. Beginning repeatedly with "my son," these passages poignantly depict the lure of sexual sin: "For the lips of a forbidden woman drip honey, and her speech is smoother than oil" (Proverbs 5:3). Here we see a parent honestly communicating the enticement of sexual sin.

Proverbs 7 is even more profound. The father graphically describes the scene: the adulteress is "dressed like a prostitute." In other words, it's clear what's for sale, and it looks good! She grabs and kisses the young fool, offering an unusual greeting, "I had to offer sacrifices, and today I have paid my vows . . ." (Proverbs 7:14). Why would she bring that up? On the surface, she knows how to talk to a man—she's explaining that she has food at home. But there's something more sinister at work. "Don't worry about all that religious stuff. I've paid my dues, we're covered. We can be good Jews who worship in the temple and do this too!" Sound familiar? It is the invitation of the devil to compartmentalize our lives, relegating faith to Sunday morning and good deeds; limiting the gospel to what happened at the altar call, not the call of our King to rule over us.

Then the adulteress says what every man longs to hear, "I want you!" and gives great detail describing the luxury of her bedroom and the sweet smell of her bed, appealing to all of his senses, promising complete satisfaction. Then she delivers the clincher, "Come, let us take our fill of love till morning; let us delight ourselves with love" (Proverbs 7:18). She is essentially saying, "I want you to take me again and again until the sun comes up!"

Why the graphic, prolonged description to a "just say, 'no'" lecture? The father is communicating something very important to his son: "This looks good! It seems foolish to pass this up." Perhaps even, "It tugs at my flesh too." He clearly communicates he understands *why* the son would be enticed. However, biblical wisdom is seeing the end from the beginning, so the father warns, "But in the end she is bitter as wormwood, sharp as a two-edged sword. Her feet go down to death; her steps follow the path to Sheol" (Proverbs 5:4–5). "All at once he follows her, as an ox goes to the slaughter, or as a stag is caught fast till an arrow pierces its liver; as a bird rushes into a snare; he does not know that it will cost him his life" (Proverbs 7:22–23). Your teens need to know that you *understand* what it's like to resist the pull of your flesh. They need to hear honestly from their parents that you are in this fight too!

Although these passages speak directly to fathers and sons, the same principles apply to mothers and daughters. Lauren Winner articulates one of the church's lies is that women don't really want sex anyway.[2] This lie must be addressed. Our daughters need more than the warning "guys only think of one thing." They need parents that will come alongside them, understand their struggle with lust, and point them to the One who gives us the grace to stand in the midst of temptation.

Are you honest with your teen about your own struggle with temptation or do you present yourself as one who is past all that? These passages urge gut-level honesty and transparency, to walk alongside our young adult children. In the first century, kids were considered adults at thirteen. We need to realize our teenage children are individuals desperate for the grace of God and in need of the community of faith to help them live a life of sexual integrity.

In addition to unprecedented levels of sexual temptation easily accessible, the web is teeming with predators trying to connect with young men and women (not to mention little children). I've spoken with many parents whose young teens were drawn into emotional and even cyber-sexual relationships online, being groomed for a physical encounter. You must take steps to wisely safeguard your kids in today's technological world. To not do so is gross neglect of your parental responsibilities. Every parent who caught their child looking at porn or entering into sexual conversation on social media would have sworn the day before that their child would *never* do such a thing! A very helpful resource is Nicholas Black's minibook, *iSnooping on Your Kid: Parenting in an Internet World.*[3]

Beyond the digital realm, sexual activity among teens is rampant and devoid of relationship as never before. The idea of "friends with benefits" has been around for years. The hook-up culture has at last brought the sexual revolution to its fullness. Young women are now as promiscuous as men, and sex is as prevalent as "making out" was a generation ago. Even among Christian teens there's confusion about what behaviors equal sexual sin. Many limit sexual sin to intercourse, permitting all kinds of other sexual activity while maintaining "virginity."

Wise parenting means addressing these challenges and (as mentioned above) acknowledging the sacrifice of obedience. It is an act of *faith!* While everyone around them is telling them to embrace life while they are young, that they're missing out if they don't, it is a supreme act of faith for your kids to believe Christ and surrender their sexuality to him.

This is an opportunity to talk about the reality that God's world works his way. There are consequences to sexual behavior outside marriage. As mentioned above, sex outside God's design is robbing yourself of his good gift. It may even be profitable to discuss the growing demographic of men in their twenties dealing with sexual dysfunction. Many young men are so "pornified" that they are incapable of performing with a real person. The phenomenon is growing such that secular researchers who care nothing about biblical morality are beginning to sound the alarm. I have worked with a number of newly married Christian men who either can't maintain arousal or must resort to fantasies to be "intimate" with their wife! Culture invites kids to explore sexuality, promising impunity. Your kids need to know this is a lie. If you have brokenness in your own past, prayerfully consider candid conversations with your teen, explaining the pain you've experienced and the challenges of "relearning" God's design for sex.

At this age, it is even more likely that your teen has gay friends at school. Helping them understand the complementarity of God's design is key. The best argument against homosexual behavior is not found in Leviticus, but Genesis 1 and 2. Help them work through the "born gay" controversy by discussing how the biblical themes of creation, fall, and redemption address the reality that everything "natural" to us sexually is broken and needs a supernatural intervention to be set right. This is true for all sexuality, not just same-sex attraction.[4] Be aware that today's Christian teens are deeply impacted by the media onslaught and the stories of their gay peers. Most are not taking a self-righteous stance, but are all too willing to change their theology to fit the spirit of the age. They need to learn God's design to understand why homosexuality doesn't "fit" any more than pornography, masturbation, or other sexual activity outside marriage.

In the midst of these conversations, realize that same-sex attraction could be an issue for your child. Do you speak about it in a way that invites their honesty? If you do have concerns and feel compelled to ask, be sure to do it in a way that doesn't label or shame them.[5]

These situations are important opportunities to help your kids learn to express their faith by discussing their own need for Christ, rather than shaking a bony finger at homosexual sinners. For too long Christians have proudly acted like we have the moral high ground in culture, and our own daily need for Christ has been lost in the conversation.

As your child ventures out to college and then adult life, the conversations should continue. Be willing to ask frank questions about the pressures they face—from both outside forces and the desires of their own hearts. The sober warnings should focus on the importance of safeguarding the treasure God has given them in their sexuality.

The Best Sex Education

The most important sex education is your own marriage! It is tragic that most parents, if sex is even addressed, simply say, "Wait until marriage." But so often teens observe their parents' relationship and say in their hearts, *Are you kidding me? Wait for that? I'm going to enjoy life while I can!*

Parents must do the hard work of cultivating deep, passionate marital intimacy to demonstrate that marriage is worth waiting for. Your life always speaks louder than your words. To a teen wrestling with the considerable challenge of raging hormones, your words will carry little weight if they do not see the fruit of a good marriage borne out in your life. Why wait if marriage doesn't look like it is worth it? Our culture teaches that marriage destroys sex. Does your marriage reflect the fallen world, where marriage is the death knell to sexuality? Or does it demonstrate that the kingdom has come and Jesus is making all things new? He enables passion and intimacy to flourish even decades into marriage! Marriage is hard. All of us have sinned against our spouse in front of our kids. But it is never too late! Commit to seeking him together in the community of faith, and as God changes your marriage, your kids will see the power of the gospel at work in your home.

Key factors to keep in mind:

- Your marriage is the best teacher for your kids.
- Start now, even if your kids are older, because it's that important!
- Start a conversation with other parents in your church to gain information and support.
- Get resources to aid your conversations.
- Pray for your children—they need your prayers as much as your encouragement and training.

Regardless of the age of your children and the regrets you may already feel, the gospel invites you to start fresh today. God's mercies are new every morning. It may seem overwhelming to discuss sexuality with your kids, but he promises to come to us daily, providing the grace for each new day's challenges. Jesus promised to never leave us or forsake us: "I will not leave you as orphans; I will come to you" (John 14:18). He is present with us by his Spirit to help us in our weakness and to bring new life to all the dead places in our relationships—if we will seek him and take the risk. Although it will put you squarely outside your comfort zone, you will never regret taking the initiative to warn of the dangers posed by fallen sexuality and to extoll the glory of God's design.

Endnotes

1. For example, listen to the Beloved's description of her Lover, "His arms are rods of gold, set with jewels. His body is polished ivory, bedecked with sapphires" (Song of Solomon 5:14). While technically accurate, it is a bit of a euphemism. A closer rendering would be: "His erection is a tusk of polished ivory, bedecked with sapphires."

2. Lauren F. Winner, *Real Sex: The Naked Truth about Chastity* (Grand Rapids: Brazos Press, 2005), 90.

3. Nicholas Black, *iSnooping on Your Kid: Parenting in an Internet World* (Greensboro, NC: New Growth Press, 2013).

4. For a fuller discussion, see David White, *Can You Change If You're Gay?* (Greensboro, NC: New Growth Press, 2013).

5. Tim Geiger, *Your Child Says "I'm Gay"* (Greensboro, NC: New Growth Press, 2013). This minibook provides practical help for navigating this kind of conversation.